WHY GOLDENS DO THAT

WHY GOLDENS DO THAT

A Collection of Curious
GOLDEN RETRIEVER Behaviors

BY TOM DAVIS

WILLOW CREEK PRESS

Published by Willow Creek Press, P.O. Box 147, Minocqua, Wisconsin 54548

Editor/Design: Andrea K. Donner

Photo credits: p.2 © Bill Silliker Jr./AnimalsAnimals; p.8 © Bonnie Nance; p.12 © Lynn Stone; p.14 © John Daniels/Ardea.com; p.16 © Cris Kelly; p.18 © Alan & Sandy Carey; p.20 © Lynn Stone; p.22 © Terry Wild Studio; p.24-26 © Lynn Stone; p.28 © Herb Segars/AnimalsAnimals; p.30 © Close Encounters of the Furry Kind; p.32 © J.&P. Wegner/AnimalsAniamls; p.34 © Norvia Behling; p.36 © Henry Holdsworth; p.38 © Norvia Behling; p.40 © J.&P. Wegner/AnimalsAnimals; p.42 © Close Encounters of the Furry Kind; p.44 © Norbert Wu/Peter Arnold Inc.; p.46 © Lynn Stone; p.48 © Bonnie Nance; p.50 © RonKimballStock.com; p.52 © Close Encounters of the Furry Kind; p.54 © Mark Raycroft/Minden Pictures; p.56 © Cris Kelly; p.58 © Mark Raycroft/Minden Pictures; p.60 © Alan & Sandy Carey; p.62 © Connie Summers; p.64 © Johan De Meester/Ardea.com; p.66 © RonKimballStock.com; p.68 © Renee Stockdale/AnimalsAnimals; p.70 © Connie Summers; p.73 © Mark Raycroft/Minden Pictures; p.74-76 © Norvia Behling; p.78 © Connie Summers; p.80-82 © Norvia Behling; p.84 © Sharon Eide/Elizabeth Flynn; p.87 © Klein/Hubert/Peter Arnold, Inc.; p.88 © RonKimballStock.com; p.90 © Henry Holdsworth; p.92 © Lynn Stone; p.94 © Close Encounters of the Furry Kind; p.96 © Ardea.com

Library of Congress Cataloging-in-Publication Data

Davis, Tom, 1956-
    Why goldens do that : a collection of curious golden
retriever behaviors / text by Tom Davis.
        p. cm.
    ISBN 1-59543-241-8 (hardcover : alk. paper)
    1. Golden retriever--Behavior--Miscellania. I. Title.
SF429.G63D38 2005
636.752'7--dc22
                                                    2005020434

Printed in Canada

Table of Contents

Introduction

As golden retrievers go she was utterly typical—even stereotypical. She lived in a middle-class suburban neighborhood: tree-lined streets, neatly clipped lawns, fenced backyards. She was a good-looking, robustly built dog (although hardly show quality), and while she wasn't a hunter I fancy she gazed with something like longing at the mallards and Canada geese that frequently flew over, en route to the nearby river. She held no titles; she achieved nothing worthy of the public record. Her distinction was all in the hearts of her family, and therefore incalculable. To them, she was as perfect as a dog could possibly be.

In other words, she was pretty much the same as 99.9 percent of all golden retrievers. I'd like to tell you a little about her—and about the two girls she helped raise.

The girls were toddlers when Ruby joined their family as a bright-eyed pup. Young women now, they can't remember ever being without her. The golden retriever named for her luxurious mahogany coat was as constant a presence in their lives as their mother and father. She'd been their playmate, romping and chasing tennis balls in the backyard, sometimes barking out of sheer exuberance; she'd been their companion on their early morning paper route, insistently nudging them awake with her soft but cold-nosed muzzle when they ached for a few more minutes of sleep. She rode with them in the car on family trips, sticking her lovely head out the window to drink in the breeze, an expression of infectiously blissful contentment on her smiling face.

But most of all, Ruby was simply there for them, letting them wrap their arms around her, sink their fingers in her soft fur, and press their cheeks against her side, feeling her breathe, smelling her warm familiar smell. Whether they wanted to share their joys, ease their sorrows, or just display affection, it made no difference. Ruby was a source of comfort and reassurance, ebullient and empathetic in equal measure. The girls loved her, unconditionally and unreservedly; she loved them back the same way.

Maybe I'm reading too much into it, but as I watched them grow into the beautiful, confident, accomplished people they are today—and I mean the kind of beauty that radiates from the inside out, not the superficial pop star kind that vanishes when the make-up's removed—it occurred to me that Ruby deserved part of the credit. Of course, they learned the lessons in responsibility that taking care of any dog teaches (any animal, for that matter). But it was hard not to think that, in a larger sense, the people they became owes something to Ruby's example. Loyalty, generosity, equanimity; responsiveness to the needs of others and willingness to give without expectation of return; the desire to make the most of every opportunity and the humility to be grateful for the good things that come your way: However the girls came to possess these qualities, the company of a certain golden retriever during the formative years of their lives sure didn't hurt.

Ruby lived to a ripe old age and, while it was a sad day when she died (the girls' dad took it hardest of all), she seemed to know it was time. With one of the girls in college and the other soon to go, it was almost as if she understood that her work was done, that there was nothing more she needed to show them, nothing more she had to give.

You raised them well, old girl. You did yourself proud. This book's for you—and for all the other golden retrievers the world has never heard of, but who have enriched our lives beyond measure.

Tom Davis
Green Bay, Wisconsin

11

Why Do Golden Retrievers Retrieve?

The canine race is blessed with a cluster of "core" behaviors that define *dog*. Many of these behaviors, such as retrieving, have proven useful to humans, and therefore humans have worked to perpetuate and enhance them. If you're thinking 'Wait a minute: Aren't goldens and the other retrieving breeds relatively recent developments?', well, in terms of the canine time-line, you're right. Dogs known as retrievers have existed only since about the 16th century, and the golden wasn't recognized as a distinct breed until the early 1900s. But dogs have *always* retrieved, for the simple reason that their wolf progenitors did (and do). When a wolf pup wanders off and Mama picks him up by the scruff of the neck, that's retrieving. Ditto when she brings food to her lit-

ter. Soon the youngsters are themselves carrying bones around and playing keep-away with their siblings. From a behavioral standpoint, it's not a huge leap from picking things up and toting them around to picking things up and bringing them back.

So it's not retrieving per se that distinguishes the golden, but the degree of desire to do it. Simply put, by selectively breeding for this trait over many generations—beginning with Lord Tweedmouth, who pretty much single-handedly developed the golden at his Scottish estate in the late-1800s—the behavior has been intensified and "fixed." A golden that truly loves to retrieve will fetch whatever you can throw—and he'll do it not only joyfully but, as your aching arm will soon attest, tirelessly, too.

Why Do Goldens Have Such Good Noses?

Much of the difficulty we have understanding canine behavior stems from a basic misapprehension, namely, that the dog's sense of smell is the same as ours, only better. Indeed, scientists have expended a lot of effort trying to quantify the difference, with estimates of the dog's olfactory superiority ranging from one thousand times better to one *million* times better. This is a misguided line of inquiry, in my opinion, because the dog's sense of smell is so unimaginably beyond ours that it's a different realm of perception. While we have around five million "scent receptors" in our schnoz, the typical golden retriever has 200-220 million. Similarly, while maybe 0.01 percent of our brain power is devoted to olfaction, 10 percent of the dog's is.

Dogs also have a specialized apparatus in the roof of the mouth, Jacobson's organ, that literally allows them to *taste* what they smell.

It's much more enlightening to compare the dog's sense of smell to our sense of sight. Dogs essentially *see* with their noses. As for the golden's special aptitude in this respect, there's abundant anecdotal evidence (and sketchy "hard" evidence) that the sense of smell is somewhat more developed in hunting breeds, although it could be that hunters are simply better at focusing and applying the olfactory powers that are every dog's birthright. As for the bedrock conviction among golden retriever partisans that their dogs have better noses than Labs do, well, I'd just as soon not go there.

Why Are Goldens So Trainable?

Who said *that*? Seriously, putting aside the question of whether you train your golden or your golden ultimately trains you— the truth lies somewhere in the middle, I suspect—goldens rank highly in terms of overall trainability. If they didn't, they wouldn't be among the top choices for guide and service dogs (see page 53).

The golden owes much of its trainability to the fact that, as a sporting dog, it's been bred for many generations to work exceptionally closely with people. It doesn't simply have to run fast, nestle comfortably in your lap, or pose attractively at the end of a leash. It has to *do a job*, a job that involves a variety of skills and functions and requires that it pay careful attention to its partner in the field (i.e., the one with two legs). Trainability, which presupposes intelligence, eagerness-to-please, and a kind of free-wheeling, lightly worn subservience, is one of the cornerstones of the relationship—and one of the hallmarks of a great hunting dog.

One caveat: Goldens tend to be "thinkers," meaning that during training you not only have to show them *what* you want them to do, you have to make them understand *why*. As long as you remember the three Ps—praise, patience, and positive reinforcement—training your golden will be a pleasant experience for both of you.

Why Do Goldens Chase Things?

Well, for one thing, if they're going to retrieve it, first they have to catch it. That sounds glib, but in reality it cuts pretty close to the heart of the matter. All dogs are born with the desire to chase. Remember, dogs are predators by nature; if you "scratch" a dog, even one as sweet-tempered and emphatically *civilized* as a golden retriever, you find a wolf. Something moves, what animal behaviorists call the "prey chase drive" is activated, and the dog takes off in hot pursuit. In the oldest, most primitive recesses of the canine brain—an area that developed long before there were such potentially hazardous creatures as Buicks, Pontiacs, and Chevrolets—if it appears to be running away, it must be food. And if it's food, says this part of the dog's brain that still lives in Jurassic Park, you'd better try to catch it—because you never know when your next meal is coming.

To be sure, the intensity of the prey chase drive varies from breed to breed and individual to individual. As a hunting dog with a major in retrieving, though, it's safe to say that the golden is near the top of the class. The good news is that golden retrievers are smart and trainable enough to learn pretty quickly when it's okay to chase (if ever) and when it isn't.

Why Do Goldens Love to Swim?

Not all of them do, actually. While I've yet to see a golden that was genuinely *afraid* of water, I've seen a few that entered it with obvious displeasure. They were decent swimmers, too. Like certain women of my acquaintance, they simply preferred to keep their hair from getting wet.

The vast majority of goldens, though, are as happy in the water as ducks, and they'll capitalize on any excuse, pretense, and/or opportunity to splash, swim, and generally frolic in the stuff. They're doing what comes naturally; you might even say the golden gravitates to water by genetic predisposition. Lord Tweedmouth developed the golden to be an all-purpose gun dog, and an important part of its job description was retrieving from water. It's unlikely that a dog reluctant to fetch a duck would have gotten the nod for breeding; conversely, a dog that hit the water eagerly would have been a prime candidate. Over time, this behavior became part of the breed's genetic inheritance, along with such water-friendly "adaptations" as an insulating layer of subcutaneous fat and the warm, luxuriant coat that is the golden's pride-and-joy. Swimming's a great way to cool off, too.

Why Do Goldens Pant So Much?

When dogs get hot, whether as the result of exertion, nervous anticipation, or ambient temperature, they pant. It's what dogs do to dissipate heat and regulate their internal temperature, which is normally around 101°F. The rapid movement of air across the moist surfaces of the mouth, tongue, and throat cools by evaporation. The same principle is at work when we humans sweat; it's just the mechanism that's different. Panting also functions as a rudimentary heat exchange: warm air out, cooler air in.

The reason goldens tend to pant more than a lot of dogs is that they heat up faster. The thick coat that equips them to withstand brush, briars, cold water, and the chilly conditions typical of hunting season is something of a handicap in warmer weather. Size factors into this equation as well: Simply put, larger dogs like goldens have a harder time dissipating heat—but an easier time staying warm—than smaller dogs. (It has to do with the ratio of surface area to internal area, which is why white-tailed deer in Texas, for example, are considerably smaller than their cousins in Saskatchewan.) It's worth remembering, too, that the golden is a native of Scotland, which lies at roughly the same latitude as Hudson Bay and where no one is ever far from a wool sweater.

Why Do Goldens Have Such Long Coats?

As revealed by Lord Tweedmouth's records, a wavy-coated retriever named Nous was the "foundation" for the line that eventually became the golden retriever breed. ("Wavy-coated retriever" fell out of favor in the late-1800s and was replaced by "flat-coated retriever," the name that survives today.) What made Nous unique, apart from his sterling qualities as a gun dog, is that he was yellow, not black, which is the normal color for wavy-coated/flat-coated retrievers. And while Lord Tweedmouth did add some bloodhound to the mix to improve tracking ability, Nous and the rest of the dogs that "built" the golden retriever breed, including the now-extinct Tweed water spaniel, other wavy-coats, and an Irish setter, all had long hair.

The short answer to the question, then, is that goldens have *always* had long coats. They're definitely longer now than they were originally, however, and that's because a long, luxuriant coat is such an eye-catcher that breeders, those on the "show" side in particular, have selectively emphasized this trait. Beauty has its price, of course: Can you say "burr magnet?"

Why Are Some Goldens Red and Others Blonde?

While the "classic" golden retriever coat color is a lustrous copper-gold, the breed comes in shades ranging from a rich mahogany red to a blonde so pale that it appears almost white. (It's hard to tell some of the red ones from Irish setters, and I confess to staring in bewilderment at some of the ultra-blonde ones trying to figure out *what* the heck they are—perhaps an obscure Nordic breed I'm unfamiliar with.) Part of this is accidental—attributable to the golden's "normal" genetic variation, that is—but part of it is by design. A breeder takes a fancy to a certain shade, and, in much the same way that a painter mixes colors on his palette, selects sires and dams whose coat colors will ultimately "mix" to create the desired result—the "signature" of said breeder's line or kennel.

As a general rule of thumb, the coats of goldens bred primarily for the field tend toward the red side of the color spectrum, while the coats of those bred for the bench tend to fall toward the yellow end. In other words, if you're looking for a hunting companion, think Rita Hayworth or Maureen O'Hara; if you're looking to win Best in Show, Grace Kelly would probably be a better bet.

Why Do Goldens Shed So Much?

The writer Gene Hill, who had a profound love for dogs, once penned an essay called something like "Dog Hair in Your Drink." The point was that anyone who visited the Hill home should expect to find dog hair in his or her libation, and that anyone who complained about it, or even bothered to mention it, was welcome not to return. They sure as hell weren't going to be *invited* back.

The larger moral was that if a little surplus dog hair gets under your skin, you can't by definition be a dog person. You definitely can't be a golden retriever person, because their abundant coat arguably makes them the leaders of the whole pack when it comes to shedding. You can brush a golden until your hands bleed, but during the annual spring/summer "molt" you might as well resign yourself to a seemingly infinite exfoliation of tufts, clumps, and random airborne fibers—like leaves falling in the autumn woods, and about as easy to keep up with.

In terms of *why*, shedding serves a couple of purposes. One is that, by getting rid of the old, dead, used-up hair, it promotes new growth—pretty much the same way that raking the "thatch" from your lawn reinvigorates the grass. The other is that it outfits dogs with a wardrobe appropriate to the season: lighter and cooler in the summer, heavier and warmer in the winter. It's just that when goldens switch over to their summer ensemble, there's an awful lot of winter stuff to get rid of.

Why Do Goldens Enjoy Being Brushed?

Because it feels darn good, that's why. To a golden retriever, I imagine that being brushed feels kind of like a scalp massage feels to us, all tingly and soothing and so euphorically, stimulatingly *wonderful* that you don't want it to end. Ever. If you want to accuse me of anthropomorphizing, fine—but how, then, do you explain the look of enraptured bliss a golden retriever invariably wears when it's getting a thorough brushing?

Part of the pleasure—for the dog, I mean—is undoubtedly the attention that comes with being fussed over; as we all know, goldens soak up attention the way loamy soil soaks up rain. The basic physical contact is another component, along with the brushing motion itself, which may stir puppyhood memories of being licked by their dam. Lastly, I'm convinced that it simply feels good to dogs—especially when they have the copious amount of hair a golden retriever has—to be relieved of some of the "excess." Left to their own devices, after all, dogs will accomplish this themselves by finding a rough surface—a chain-link fence, for example—to rub against.

Why Do Goldens Come in "Big-boned" and "Small-boned" Versions?

Over the years, many of the sporting breeds—including the golden retriever—have split into two broad "types": a field or hunting type and a show/pet type. Breeders of the former contend that the bench standard is based on an arbitrary standard of beauty that gives scant consideration to the qualities necessary to perform in the field. Form does not follow function in the show ring, goes this argument, but is instead exalted for its own sake. The show crowd, while acknowledging there may be some truth to this, wonder why the field breeders (some of them, at least) have gone so far in the other direction, virtually ignoring conformation. I used to kid a couple friends of mine, both extremely serious hunters who owned littermate goldens of less-than-classic appearance, that their dogs looked "a little like golden retrievers." They themselves referred to them, not without affection, as "swamp collies."

So when you see a smallish, relatively fine-boned golden, chances are it's from a long line of hunters. When you see a bigger, bulkier individual, it's likely a product of show stock—although every once in a while you run across a golden of size and substance that can still cut it in the field. Would that there were more.

Why Do Goldens Like to Chew on Things?

In fairness, goldens have no monopoly on this behavior. Puppies chew furniture, shoes (the funkier-smelling the better), gloves, anything made of leather or animal hide, and, well, pretty much whatever they can get their jaws around because it helps them shed their needle-sharp puppy teeth and allows their adult dentition to grow in. For older dogs, gnawing on bones and "chew toys" is nature's way of keeping their teeth clean and their gums healthy. In the wild, a good set of choppers is a tremendous advantage for a predator species; the ancestral wolves that settled in for long, leisurely bone-chewing sessions, in addition to extracting every milli-calorie of food value, gave themselves an edge in the oral hygiene department and were therefore better equipped to survive and reproduce—thus incorporating the behavior into the genetic mother board of the canine race.

It does seem true, however, that goldens are more apt to chew and "mouth" than a lot of dogs. A dog's mouth is essentially its "hands," doubly so for a retrieving breed, and I'm convinced that goldens (Labs too, for that matter) derive an almost tactile pleasure from the feel of certain objects in their mouths. That's my theory, anyway, and I'm sticking to it.

Why Do Goldens Yip and Twitch While Sleeping?

We're all familiar with this: our dogs twitching, jerking, "paddling," yipping, whimpering, woofing, and so on while sound asleep. It's often kind of comical—also goofily endearing—and putting two-and-two together from our own experience we assume they must be having a particularly vivid dream: chasing a cat up a tree, romping in the park with the kids, or flushing a big rooster pheasant, for example. Which is exactly what's happening, although the science that proves it is of fairly recent vintage. After all, it's not as if you can wake up a dog, even one as communicative as a golden retriever, and ask him to relate the details of his dream.

The phase of sleep in which dogs twitch, yip, etc., is known as rapid eye movement (REM) sleep. If you compare an EEG reading taken during REM sleep with one taken while the dog is fully awake, the results are almost identical. What scientists have concluded from this is that dogs are *conscious* during REM sleep, which leads me to ponder the unanswerable question of whether they're able to distinguish between their "dream" life and their "real" life. (As if we humans invariably have a firm grasp on that.) Another really interesting thing is that during REM sleep the large voluntary muscles are essentially paralyzed—the reason dogs merely twitch instead of galloping around the room bouncing off walls, furniture, and what have you.

Why Do Goldens Sometimes "Raise Their Hackles"?

Unlike humans, who for the most part only "bristle" metaphorically—when we're insulted, for example—goldens bristle literally, raising the hair on their neck, shoulders, spine, rump, even the top of their tail in response to perceived threats. The technical term for this is *piloerection*, from the Latin word for hair, *pilus*. Piloerection occurs in humans, too, of course: The hair on our arms stands up in response to cold, and the hair on the back of our necks stands up when we're afraid.

There are a couple of important differences, though. One is that dogs rarely raise their hackles in response to outside temperature. Instead, the behavior is a reflection of the dog's *emotional* temperature when it finds itself in a situation it perceives as threatening. Most commonly, the behavior manifests itself during encounters with other dogs. By looking larger and more imposing, the "hackled up" individual tries to assert its dominance and convince the "challenger" to back off, thereby avoiding a physical confrontation. The kicker is that sometimes raised hackles are indicative of a more fearful, submissive attitude, which is why to interpret the meaning correctly you have to read it in the context of the dog's overall body language.

This brings us to the other important difference between canine and human piloerection: To a certain extent dogs, unlike people, are able to control it.

Why Do Goldens Have So Much Energy?

The writer Jim Harrison (a dog lover of the highest order, coincidentally) speculates that the reason the French consume astonishing quantities of cheese, butter, and cream but have a relatively low incidence of heart disease has less to do with drinking red wine and walking every day than it does with this: Because they believe they're superior to pretty much everybody else, the French possess very little of the existential *angst* that plagues the rest of mankind and renders us susceptible to all manner of stress-related afflictions.

This same general theory explains why golden retrievers have such an abundance of energy. Not that they necessarily think they're better than other dogs—although I have a hunch some of them do—but that they're so blissfully *unencumbered*. They never feel, as we often do, that the weight of the world is on their shoulders; they neither dwell on the mistakes of the past nor on the uncertainties of the future—to say nothing of the myriad grinding pressures (job, spouse, kids, ad. inf.) that wrack us on a daily basis. Thus, they live their lives with an infectiously buoyant *joie de vivre*, their paws barely touching the ground, ready and willing to seize the day and make the most of every opportunity. The good news is that some of their enthusiasm invariably rubs off on *us*.

Why Do Goldens Smile So Much— or Do They Just Look Like They're Smiling?

No dyed-in-the-fur golden "person" would add the qualifier to the end of that question, because it would never occur to such a person that his or her beloved dogs were doing anything *but* smiling. I suppose you could argue that it's to some extent a learned behavior, that goldens, being highly intelligent, figure out right quick that the more they smile, the more attention, affection, praise, and various and sundry "rewards" they receive. But this strikes me as cynical, and it ignores the crucial fact that dogs in general—and goldens in particular—are terrible actors. And even worse liars. Certainly some dogs are more or less stoic, or more or less "reactive,"

than others, but with goldens what they show is how they feel. They're not dissemblers; they can't be duplicitous, sly, or even coy. If they're smiling, it's because they're happy, damnit. And if they're happy, there's no reason you shouldn't be, too.

Of course, this begs the question of why goldens *are* so darn happy. Partly, this can be explained on the same grounds as the previous question. But it's also the case that it's simply their nature, for which we owe an unpayable debt of gratitude to Lord Tweedmouth and the many dedicated breeders who followed him, shaping, molding, and refining the golden retriever into the paragon of personality we know and adore today.

Why Do Goldens Love To Play?

Zoologists who have studied the development of the dog—and, in particular, the critical changes that served to distinguish it morphologically and behaviorally from the wolf—use the word "neoteny" a lot. What this fancy-sounding term refers to is the retention of juvenile characteristics into adulthood—and what the zoologists have concluded is that in some ways dogs never grow up. In other words, they're perpetual puppies. As Temple Grandin puts it in *Animals in Translation*, "Adult dogs look more like wolf puppies than like wolf adults and act more like wolf puppies than wolf adults, too. That's because dogs *are* wolf puppies: *genetically, dogs are juvenile wolves.*" She adds, "Humans got along best with submissive, puppy-like wolves, and over time that's what they got..."

But just as surely as all dogs are puppies (no matter how grown-up a facade they present to the world), golden retrievers are the canine race's definitive Peter Pans. Oh, they can be as serious as the next dog when there's a job to do, but once the five o'clock whistle blows they're ready to cut loose and kick up their heels. They simply seem to have an unlimited and inexhaustible capacity for *fun*, to which there's really nothing more to say except this: Lucky us!

Why Do Goldens Crave—and Display— So Much Affection?

It goes back to this concept of neoteny—and to the pack dynamic that governs so much of the social behavior of wolves and, therefore, dogs. The typical golden retriever's "pack," of course, is its human family. And, assuming this family functions more-or-less normally, the dog occupies a subordinate, subservient role. (There are some families that have yielded the Alpha position to the dog, but it's usually a little yappy dog with a Napoleon complex, as opposed to one with the positive self-image and refreshing absence of "issues" that characterize the golden retriever.)

In any event, when you combine the golden's almost reverential attitude toward its superiors in the pack with its neotenized (i.e., puppy-like) need for affirmation and positive reinforcement, what you get is an insatiable appetite for affection. But goldens have such an innate generosity and sense of gratitude that they don't hoard the sugar. Instead, they give it back as good as they get it—if not better. As one wag put it, while goldens and people may not have invented the mutual admiration society, they almost certainly perfected it.

Why Do Goldens Have Such Sweet Dispositions?

You might as well ask why the sun comes up. There's a sense in which this attribute is self-perpetuating: All else equal, the dogs with the most attractive personalities are the likeliest to be used for breeding, and when you breed one individual with a pleasing temperament to another, chances are the pups will prove "true to type," as the serious dog folks say.

But it's also, as alluded to previously, a reflection of the golden's fundamental emotional and psychological soundness—which, in turn (as also alluded to previously), stems from its status not just as a sporting breed, but as a *working gun dog*. The attentiveness, the eagerness-to-please, and the boundless enthusiasm and equanimity prized by hunters—the building blocks of personality, in short—became as much the hallmarks of the breed as its prowess as a retriever or its elegant coat. And they continue to go a long way toward explaining the golden's popularity among dog lovers of *every* stripe. Which is not to say that they don't get surly or snarky on occasion, or that their tolerance for provocation is infinite. Even a golden retriever has a breaking point.

Why Do Goldens Enjoy "Kissing" People?

Make no mistake: When goldens lick our faces—frenziedly, deliberately, or somewhere in-between—they are indeed kissing us. What is kissing, anyway, but an oral display of affection? And we all know that a golden misses an opportunity to display affection about as often as a politician misses an opportunity to get his mug in front of a camera.

Given how profoundly scent-oriented the canine race is in general, I think goldens are initially drawn to our faces because of the bouquet of interesting aromas emanating therefrom. (Ditto with our, um, "nether" regions; see page 81.) I mean, if dogs could talk, they'd undoubtedly be able to list every foodstuff you've consumed in the previous 24 hours, or at least since you last flossed your teeth. To say nothing of any microscopic crumbs or smears adhering to your lips, chin, beard, etc. Remember: Dogs can detect scent in the parts-per-billion range, or better, so it doesn't take much to get their attention. Then there's your breath, which dogs always seem to enjoy a lot more than other people do. (Go figure.) So it could be that their first tentative "kisses" are really more on the order of explorations. But then, when we react with delight—as we invariably do—they figure out in a hurry that this is, as the most famous guest of a certain West Virginia correctional institution would say, a Good Thing.

Why Do Goldens Make Such Good Guide and Service Dogs?

We've already touched on some of the reasons: intelligence, trainability, eagerness to please, sound temperament, a predisposition to "partner" with people, the ability to *focus*, etc. Another reason is the golden's paw-in-glove combination of all-purpose athleticism and robustly functional conformation. Serving as a guide or service dog is physically demanding work, work that often requires a certain amount of size, strength, and even tenacity. The golden may not be the fastest or the biggest or the most agile, but in terms of the ability to perform a wide variety of tasks at a high level of competence, it's awfully tough to beat. No matter how dire or extreme the circumstances, the golden has the right stuff to respond appropriately.

Something else that's critically important to note is that the golden retriever is one of the very few breeds classified as "low fear" *and* "low aggression." Usually when a dog is deemed low in one of these characteristics, it's high in the other, and vice-versa. Low fear/low aggression translates into a dog better able to keep a cool head in confusing, unfamiliar, or stressful situations—a fairly desirable quality in guide and service animals. And when you hitch the golden's high prey drive to the harness along with these other traits, you have a dog that's an outstanding candidate for search-and-rescue work, drug and bomb detection, the list goes on.

Why Do Goldens Hunt Upland Birds as Well as Waterfowl?

These days we tend to think of any breed with "retriever" in its name as a dog whose first and highest calling is—or was, originally—fetching ducks and geese. But this is a bit of a misconception. Although it's true of the Chesapeake Bay retriever—the name alone suggests it was engineered for water work—the job description for the other retrieving breeds is much broader. The golden, in particular, was developed as an all-purpose gun dog, a dog capable not only of retrieving downed game from land or water but of flushing birds such as pheasants, grouse, and partridge from cover and, in wing-shooting parlance, "putting them before the gun." According to retriever authority Richard Wolters, the "father" of the golden retriever, Lord Tweedmouth, infused Irish setter blood into the line with the specific intention of improving the nascent breed's ability in this respect.

In other words, upland bird hunting is part of the golden's genetic blueprint. There's virtually no doubt that goldens spend more days in a typical year hunting pheasants than they do any other quarry, and with good reason: They excel at it.

Why Do Goldens Do Less Well Than Labs in Retrieving Competitions?

In the early years of American retriever field trials—the 1930s and '40s—goldens and Labs, both of which had just begun to enter this country in numbers from Great Britain, competed on a more-or-less equal basis. But this soon changed, and these days Labradors comprise the overwhelming majority of entries in recognized field trials. A handful of goldens keep things interesting—and keep Labs from dominating the competitive scene entirely.

It's not that Labs are "better" retrievers, or—heaven forbid!—that they're more intelligent. Instead, it's largely a matter of the nature of field trials themselves, which have become so demanding and complex, with the winners decided by such microscopically narrow margins, that they effectively "select" for dogs that can take an incredible amount of what trainers somewhat euphemistically refer to as "pressure." And the bottom line, for a field trialer, is that Labs can take more pressure than goldens can. It's really a matter of temperament and personality; as one wag put it, while you'd want a tough-minded, all-business Labrador to handle your money, you'd want a fun-loving golden to throw your party.

Why Do Goldens Love Going for Walks?

While there's certainly a spectrum between "resolute homebody" and "inveterate roamer," all dogs seem to have an innate curiosity about the world around them. They enjoy exploring, taking in the sights, sounds, and, most significantly, the smells. Goldens in particular are highly social, so for them it's a chance to renew old acquaintances and make new ones. And, beyond that, simply to feel the comfort that comes in the presence of familiar landmarks and to take note of what's changed for future reference. Dogs like to know what's going on, in short, and walks are their way of keeping up with current events.

While it's no longer a matter of life or death, I think a good case can be made that our dogs' enthusiasm for getting out and circulating, even if it's "on leash," springs from the same impulse that sends wolves on regular patrols of their territories. Knowledge is strength, and curiosity is nature's way of ensuring that *Canis lupus* and its principal subspecies, our friend *familiaris*, don't fall behind in their studies.

Dogs enjoy the exercise, too, of course, and there's also the opportunity walks afford simply to spend quality time with *you*, i.e., the Alpha member of the pack. You lucky dog, you.

Why Do Goldens Enjoy Riding in Cars and Hanging Their Heads Out the Window?

Like going for a walk, riding in the car is an opportunity to get out and explore the world. (You probably drive a minivan or SUV if you own a golden, so I'm using "car" generically.) Even if it's nothing more cosmic than picking up the kids at school, what's "same old, same old" to you is high adventure to your dog. The chance to spend time with you and the other members of its pack is, again, another attraction; so is the fact that the alternative is being left at home. And no golden retriever worth his kibble wants *that*. Can you say "fate worse than death?"

As far as hanging their heads out the window, you have to remember that scent is the canine race's primary means of apprehending the world and making sense of their environment. In other words, dogs "see" with their noses. And a dog in a car with the windows up is like a person in a dark room. Sticking a head out the window, conversely, or for that matter just wedging a nose into the crack, is the equivalent of flipping on the floods and getting a technicolor rush of images, perceptions, and sensory data. It also looks really cool, and given that golden retrievers have a keen sense of style—for some reason I always associate them with Ralph Lauren—I'm convinced they relish the chance to be seen in such a flattering light. Goldens subscribe to the theory *If you've got it, flaunt it.*

Why Do Goldens Rebel When They're Between One and Two Years Old?

Because they're essentially teenagers then, that's why. And if you've had the pleasure (sic) of living with a teenager, I needn't say more—because whatever I say will be old news to you. *We* were never moody, argumentative, disrespectful, irresponsible, etc., at that age, but when you get up to do chores at five a.m. and then walk 14 miles to school through waist-deep snow with nothing to eat but a turnip, as we all did back then, I suppose it has a way of taking the edge off. But these pampered, coddled, hooked-on-MTV kids today... It's a world gone mad, I tell you, mad!

The good news—and I mean *really* good news—is that our dogs' "teenage years" only last a year or so. What's happening is that they're asserting their independence, but while it expresses itself as rebellion—ignoring commands that they formerly obeyed, even willfully misbehaving—there's a lot of confusion and insecurity roiling beneath the surface. The adolescent dog is trying to grow up and adopt its adult persona—but it's not quite ready to give up its carefree puppy privileges, either. It's "conflicted," to use that pop psychology buzzword. You need to remain patient, and, in particular, *not blame yourself*. The golden retriever may be the most agreeable and easy-going of dogs, but this doesn't mean it'll never push the boundaries—or try to jerk your chain.

Why Do Adult Goldens Sometimes Refuse Commands?

Many people used to believe that dogs are merely complex machines—automatons, if you will. These days, of course, we know that dogs are able to reason, weigh options, choose a course of action, and exercise a certain amount of free will. In short, they can *think*. And, its happy-go-lucky persona notwithstanding, the golden retriever is a thinker. It shouldn't come as much of a surprise, then, if every so often your golden ignores the you-know-what out of you. He may be doing something else that's more rewarding, he may simply not be in the mood, or he may have decided that what you're asking him to do is really, really stupid and you obviously don't know what the hell you're talking about.

All else equal, dogs in confusing or stressful situations are likelier to refuse commands. In these instances, the dog typically displays an "avoidance behavior," such as retreating to a place where it feels safe. Other common expressions of avoidance include sitting or lying down, standing stock-still (usually with a low, limp tail), yawning, not making eye contact, and simply feigning interest in things you know darn well it has no interest in. The most picturesque avoidance behavior I've ever heard of was, as it happens, displayed by a golden. Apparently overwhelmed by the pressure at a field trial, he refused a command to retrieve by rolling onto his back and doing his best imitation of Old Faithful.

Why Do Goldens Sometimes Display Aggression Toward Other Dogs?

As previously noted, goldens rank low on the aggression scale—and high on the never met a stranger, *Hey Buddy, how ya doin'?* scale. If goldens were people (which they *think* they are, of course) they'd be salespersons *nonpareil*, the kind who could sell ice to Eskimos and sand to Saudis. The flip side of this coin is that their aptitude as watch dogs leaves a lot to be desired, goldens being inclined to greet intruders like long-lost relatives.

By the same token, goldens rarely display aggression toward other dogs unless they're literally backed into a corner. Every so often, though, a seemingly well-adjusted golden begins exhibiting aggressive behavior for no discernible reason, lashing out at dogs doing nothing more provocative than trying to exchange a greeting or occupying "its" space. An injury, especially if it involves the spinal column, can sometimes trigger such a response: The dog's in pain, and the thought of being jostled is more than it can bear. A violent outburst may also be symptomatic of possessiveness and insecurity vis-à-vis its owner. As animal behaviorist Dr. Patricia McConnell of the *Calling All Pets* radio show puts it, "They view their owner as a giant bone—and they're not sharing." Territoriality and dominance issues can fuel this toxic fire, too. Fortunately, few residents of the canine psych ward fit the golden's description.

Why Are Goldens Distrustful of Some Strangers and Not Others?

Again, goldens tend to recognize *no one* as a stranger and everyone as a friend (or at least a potential friend), hence their lack of employment in the guard dog business. Like all dogs and for that matter pretty much the whole animal planet, though, goldens are guilty of inductive reasoning—that is, reasoning from the part to the whole. In other words, if a person of certain physical characteristics mistreats your dog or even threatens it in a way that makes an impression, your dog is apt to regard all people of similar appearance with suspicion. It's the equivalent of what we call racial profiling, essentially. The wild card that we dim-witted humans tend to forget about is the extent to which dogs perceive the world through their noses, meaning that a person who looks completely different from a known "bad guy"—but perhaps wears the same cologne or deodorant—will set off the alarms as well.

In nature, of course, there's very little survival value in viewing an animal capable of eating you as an individual rather than as a representative of a certain class. You can scratch all the lions you want to, but you won't find a lamb underneath. Wolves brought this better-safe-than-lunch philosophy with them when they became dogs—which is why even golden retrievers, by consensus the friendliest and most amiable tribe in the canine race, occasionally give strangers the hairy eyeball.

Why Do Goldens Seem Able to Read Our Minds and Respond to Our Moods?

I've long maintained that no breed is as reliably and deeply *simpatico* as the golden retriever. If you're not familiar with it, *simpatico* is an Italian word (also a Spanish one) akin to our "sympathetic," but with a more active, participatory connotation. It perfectly describes the golden's ability to tune into our emotional wavelength and give us exactly what we need: a boisterous greeting, a nudge of the muzzle, a soulful look, a stick proffered as an invitation to play—the list goes on. Is it any surprise, then, that the golden is among the most popular therapy dogs, giving comfort to the aged, infirm, and alone, serving as a vessel into which men and women

subject to the most intense emotional stress—firefighters, police, EMTs—can unashamedly pour their grief?

It's often said that dogs can "sense" our moods, and in a way that's probably true. Emotional turmoil is often expressed physiologically, and if the hard-boiled dicks in detective novels can "smell fear," I have no doubt whatsoever that dogs, with their unimaginably superior noses, can smell certain moods. It's also the case that dogs, as borne out by a recent study at Harvard, have an uncanny knack for correctly interpreting visual "cues" from humans: reading our body language, picking up on subtle—but telling—inflections of voice, manner, and carriage. The researchers found that dogs are vastly better at this than wolves are, leading them to conclude that there has been "direct selection for dogs with the ability to read social cues in humans."

Which explains why, 15,000 years later, our golden retrievers can read us like an open book.

Why Do Goldens Eat Grass?

Because all dogs do. The $64,000 question is, do dogs get sick and throw up because they eat grass, or do they eat grass because they feel sick and *want* to throw up? And the answer is, Yes.

What you have to remember is that dogs are carnivores by nature, but omnivores by necessity and circumstance. When their wolf forebears brought down a moose, deer, caribou, or any of the large herbivores that comprised the bulk of their diet, they immediately tore into the paunch, consuming not only the flesh and organs but vegetable matter in various states of digestion. Over time, the canine race developed a taste for the stuff. Our dogs' desire for an occasional "green salad," then, is an atavistic expression of something deep within their racial memory. The thing no one really has a good explanation for is why this desire seems strongest in the springtime, when the grass is in the first vibrant flush of growth. Maybe it's just particularly succulent then, although I suspect that simple opportunity—our dogs are "on the rebound" following a winter of deprivation—has quite a bit to do with it.

The problem, as every dog owner knows, is that grass doesn't stay down. Dogs don't have the right enzymes to digest the stuff, which is why there's typically a cause-and-effect relationship between grass-eating and upchucking.

Why Do Goldens Sometimes Eat Poop?

I've said it before and I'll say it again: Dogs, even highly refined, aristocratic dogs like the golden retriever, are blissfully unaffected by the Fear of Excrement that haunts mankind. The reason for this is that their wolf forebears figured out that if the alternative was death by starvation, gnoshing on just about anything with nutritive value—including, if necessary, excrement—made a lot of sense. Speaking from personal experience, there's a sort of pyramid of disgust, with cow pies, horse apples, and various wild scat (deer, rabbits, etc.) at the bottom, the stools of other dogs in the middle, their own stools (gak!) occupying the penultimate level, and at the gross-out apex—drumroll, please—cat poop filched from the litter box. Now *that's* disgusting.

It's thought that one of the reasons dogs eat their own waste is that they're imitating what they see us doing when we pick up after them. And because dogs pick things up with their mouths… You get the picture. Another theory is that dogs that have been disciplined for defecating "inappropriately" may scarf poop in an effort to cover their tracks and escape further reprimands. Anxiety, stress, and boredom, especially in dogs confined to kennels for extended periods, probably contribute to this behavior as well.

Why Do Goldens Roll in Offal, Carrion, and Other Putrid Stuff?

This one's always a puzzler for the average owner, who wonders how an animal with such a sensitive nose can take such delight in smearing itself with the vilest, ripest, most stomach-turning gunk it can find. But it points up, yet again, the great divide between the human and canine senses of smell. It also illustrates that what comes up sevens for one species in the evolutionary crapshoot is snake-eyes for another. The aroma of rotting organic matter makes us retch because our ancestors learned, the hard way, that contact or consumption has dire consequences. Wolves, however, who had the stomach for it (literally), learned to scavenge meals when fresh meat wasn't readily available—which is why the nasty stuff apparently smells pretty good to their descendants.

As to why they relish the opportunity to roll around in it, one theory goes that it's a way to mask their scent from prey species. Not that the typical golden has to roam the 'burbs hunting for supper, but when the behavior's encoded in the genes there's no stopping it. Another theory posits that it's a way for dogs to keep a record of their travels. As Elizabeth Marshall Thomas notes in *The Hidden Life of Dogs*, a dog smeared with stinky goo is viewed by its peers as a storyteller, and canine society holds storytellers in high esteem. The person charged with bathing one of these bards is likely to have his own thoughts on the matter.

Why Do Goldens Stick Their Noses in People's Crotches?

Here's a candidate for Life's Most Embarrassing Moment: You invite your boss, clergyman, or other VIP for an elegant dinner—and no sooner does he/she step through the door than your golden plants its big wet nose right in their, um, herbarium. If the individual on the receiving end knows dogs, no apology is necessary. Otherwise, all you can do is attempt to explain that this is the canine race's way of saying "Hello!" and "Have we met before?"—and that it's in no way a commentary on the recipient's personal hygiene.

Dogs stick their noses in our crotches for the same reason they sniff one another's rear ends, a.k.a. "inguinal areas": to establish identity. Every dog has a unique "scent signature" created by its anal glands, a signature that distinguishes it from other dogs, tells whether it's male or female, and probably conveys additional information as well. The long and short of it, then, is that the anatomical nether region, with its bouquet of intriguing aromas, is where a dog in search of answers naturally gravitates. It's also the case that the muzzle of most golden retrievers and the crotch of the average person happen to occupy about the same level. "Locational inevitability," you might call it.

Why Do Goldens Beg For Food?

Because we let them. Or, more accurately, because we tacitly *encourage* them, slipping them tidbits from the table when we think no one's looking. There could hardly be a better, clearer example of what behavioral scientists call a "positive feedback loop": Dog sits next to your chair, its soulful brown eyes gazing imploringly up at yours (or, even worse, dog rests its head on your thigh), and at some point during the performance a cube of sirloin finds its way from your plate to your hand to the dog's mouth. Thus rewarded, dog's inclination to beg is reinforced, and the "poor, poor, pitiful me" act starts all over again. If not a monster, exactly, you've created a heck of a skillful panhandler.

As long as it doesn't constitute a nuisance or become disruptive—in which case you'll probably have to crate, kennel, or otherwise sequester your dog until you finish eating—a little begging's nothing to get worked up about. What you really have to stay on top of is its effect on your dog's weight. That layer of subcutaneous fat that helps insulate goldens from cold water can turn into a layer of bona fide blubber if your dog's ingesting more calories than it's burning off, and an obese dog runs the same gauntlet of health risks an obese person does: cardiovascular disease, diabetes, joint and skeletal problems, et. al. If you want to slip your dog the occasional goodie, fine—just don't give him a steady diet of the stuff.

Why Do Goldens Dig Holes and Bury Bones?

All canids have a predisposition to dig. Pound-for-pound, the champion diggers are the terriers, which makes perfect sense when you consider that the name "terrier" derives from the Latin word for earth, *terra* (as in terra firma, terra incognita, terrestrial, etc.), and that terriers were known in antiquity as "earth dogges." The terrier breeds were developed to follow game "to ground"—that is, to the critter's hole, tunnel, or burrow—and, if necessary, dig their way in. The digging instinct was always there, of course; wolves dig to root out food, excavate dens, and even create a cool place to lie down, and because the ability to dig contributed to survival it became incorporated at the genetic level. Selective breeding simply intensified the digging behavior in terriers, just as it did the desire to retrieve in goldens.

But if goldens are also-rans in the grand scheme of canine digging, the fact that they're large, strong, and determined means that when they *do* get a Jones to dig they can cause serious damage. Digging in goldens is typically a sign of boredom and surplus nervous energy, so if your dog's making the backyard look like a cratered World War I battlefield you should try to give him more exercise. It'll do you both good.

Oh, and as for burying bones, that's called "caching"—putting surplus food in a safe place for later consumption. It's basically the same thing squirrels do when they bury acorns in the fall. Not that your golden needs to worry about where it's next meal is coming from, but there's a place in all dogs' brains where the wolf still howls—and where *nothing* is taken for granted.

Why Do Goldens Bark and Sometimes Howl?

The funny thing about barking is that while wolves *can* bark, they almost never do. This has led scientists to theorize that humans cultivated barking in the domestic dog because it proved useful to them. A dog that "sounded the alarm" at the approach of danger was a valuable commodity, indeed. Over time, as the barkers were selected for breeding, the behavior became an integral part of the dog's make-up.

Dogs, including goldens, still bark to issue a challenge to intruders, but these days they bark for a lot of other reasons as well: as an invitation to play, as an expression of exuberance or boredom, because they want something. I've even known several hunting goldens that would bark when a grouse they flushed lit in a tree. The bottom line is that barking is perhaps the dog's primary means of communicating with humans, the canine race having discovered long ago that people, with their blunted senses, don't respond very well to methods that work perfectly well with other dogs, such as scent signals and body language.

Howling, on the other hand, *is* one of the ways canids communicate with one another. Among golden retrievers, though, howling is hit-or-miss at best, with some indulging regularly and others not at all. In the cities and suburbs—the golden's natural habitat—the majority of howling is in response to the wail of a police, fire, or ambulance siren.

Why Do Goldens Spend So Much Time Napping?

Define "so much time." By the standards of Americans, who wear their sleep deprivation like a badge of honor, anyone who grabs more than five hours of shut-eye in a given 24-hour period is either a hopeless slacker or was recently discharged from the hospital following heart-bypass surgery. As far as napping during the day is concerned, you might as well confess to mugging little old ladies or stealing from the offering plate at church. This brings me to Jim Harrison's observation that most of the "fatal mischief" at large in the world is the work of non-nappers, people "who can't leave well enough alone."

The reason goldens nap, then, is that it's their first line of defense against the impulse to do mischief (fatal or otherwise), stick their noses into places where noses shouldn't be stuck, and create problems where none previously existed. I'm also convinced that nappers, canine or human, tend to be pleasant, agreeable, easy-going, and even-tempered, while non-nappers tend to be moody, irritable, high-strung, and simply not much fun to be around. I don't have to tell you which category better describes the golden retriever. If they're hunting, working, or playing, they can go all day. If not, they're perfectly content to romp the fields of Dreamland. More power to them.

Why Do Goldens Love Us Despite Our Faults?

Because dogs in general, and golden retrievers in particular, have an almost unlimited capacity to forgive. Without getting too theological about it, the creation, development, and refinement of the various dog breeds has allowed man to play God, tweaking and tinkering to suit our own purposes. Thankfully, we did not create the dog in our *own* image, but in an idealized and some might say godly version of it, one imbued with the qualities we strive to embody but, being human, all too often fail to exhibit: courage, loyalty, devotion, selflessness, patience, perseverance, unwavering good humor, ad. inf. And, of course, a well of unconditional love so profound that its depths cannot be plumbed by any instrument, nor even fathomed by the imagination. Our dogs' example shames us—and inspires us to do better.

So, while we're miserable, undeserving wretches most of the time, our goldens continue to adore us, freely and happily giving far more than they get in return. It defies logical explanation, really—but what a gift, and what a blessing, it is.

Why Do Goldens Risk Their Lives to Save Their Masters?

At the risk of sounding like a broken record (not that anyone born after about 1980 knows what that sounds like), it's in large part because of the qualities mentioned in the previous answer: courage, loyalty, devotion, selflessness, the list goes on. A golden retriever that sees a member of its human family—its pack, if you will—in desperate straits can no sooner *not* try to help than it can refuse the juiciest steak in Texas after going without food for a week. Some argue that dogs put themselves so willingly in harm's way because they have no foreknowledge of death, and are thus unburdened of the fears and anxieties that are the toxic by-products of that knowledge. But dogs have a fierce survival instinct, too, and there are situations—entering a burning building, for example—in which they're almost certainly aware they're putting their lives on the line. That they do it anyway, without hesitation, only underscores their inherent nobility.

And it's just what golden retrievers—partners, best friends, boon companions—do.